Festive
Coffee Shop Drinks

Festive
Coffee Shop
Drinks

MORE THAN 50 HOLIDAY-INSPIRED RECIPES
FOR COFFEES, HOT CHOCOLATES & MORE

WITH RECIPES BY
HANNAH MILES

WITH PHOTOGRAPHY BY
ALEX LUCK

RYLAND PETERS & SMALL
LONDON • NEW YORK

For my fiancée John, who slurped all the milkshakes, love you xxx

Senior Designer Toni Kay
Editorial Director Julia Charles
Creative Director Leslie Harrington
Production Manager
  Gordana Simakovic

Food Stylist Lorna Brash
Prop Stylist Luis Peral
Indexer Hilary Bird

First published in 2023 by
Ryland Peters & Small
20–21 Jockey's Fields
London WC1R 4BW
and Ryland Peters & Small, Inc.
341 East 116th Street
New York NY 10029

www.rylandpeters.com

ISBN: 978-1-78879-554-8

10 9 8 7 6 5 4 3 2 1

Printed and bound in China

CIP data from the Library of Congress has been applied for. A CIP record for this book is available from the British Library.

NOTES
* Both British (metric) and American measurements (imperial plus US cups) are included; do not to alternate between the two within a recipe.
* All spoon measurements are level unless specified otherwise. Note that a level tablespoon (tbsp) is 15 ml and a level teaspoon (tsp) is 5 ml.
* To sterilize screwtop jars or bottles, preheat the oven to 160°C/150°C fan/325°F/gas 3. Wash the vessels and their lids in hot soapy water then rinse but don't dry them. Remove rubber seals, put the jars on a baking sheet and into the oven for 10 minutes. Soak the lids in boiling water for a few minutes before using.

Contents

Introduction

There are people who count the days until the first release of the festive-themed drinks menu at their local coffee shop and I am definitely one of those people. I know it is time to start the Christmas countdown when I take my first sip of a spicy gingerbread latte and, as you have bought this book, I expect you already have your own firm favourite too! I have put together a collection of deliciously festive beverages to further tempt you, with ideas for treats to make at home such as warming lattes and cappuccinos, as well as ice cream shakes, ice-blended frappés and cold brews.

In the pages that follow you will find hints and tips on how to make your coffees like a pro barista, from frothing milk to batching basic cold brew coffee. I've also included easy recipes for making coffee shop-style flavoured syrups at home. Choose from toffee nut, gingerbread and Irish cream, as well as vanilla and peppermint, plus sticky chocolate and caramel sauces which can be used to decorate latte glasses or simply drizzled over finished drinks just before serving. There are also ideas for decorating your coffees, with stencilling, feathering and even edible glitter for adding a extra little Christmas sparkle!

The Hot Coffee & Tea Drinks chapter contains all the classic coffees you might expect to find – vanilla latte, caramel macchiato and the hugely popular toffee nut latte. There are also some modern ideas to try, such as the delicious Dutch caramel stroopwafel latte, peppermint white mocha and a yummy fluffernutter latte, which combines peanut butter and toasted marshmallow fluff, inspired by the popular fluffernutter sandwich! For a sophisticated drink there is a perfumed pistachio latte and for those of who prefer dairy-free drinks why not try an almond latte or a toasted coconut latte? For an extra warming grown-up treat, sip a rum coffee with burnt sugar syrup or a boozy Caribbean coffee.

The next chapter features Mochas & Hot Chocolates inspired by candy treats such as a malt ball hot chocolate, a mega brownie hot chocolate and an orange hot chocolate. For a reminder of campfire summers, there is a s'mores hot chocolate and an autumn/fall inspired toffee apple white hot chocolate with candy apples.

In the Frappés, Shakes & Cold Brews chapter you'll find a variety of chilled treats, ideal for any Christmas holiday spent in the sunshine. For those who want a festive indulgence, the shakes in this chapter will not disappoint – there is a doughnut freakshake, a 'cereal milk' shake and a cookies and cream shake. And for a party there's also a recipe for a stylish cold brew espresso martini cocktail.

So this festive season, why not get cosy and invite friends and family over for a coffee party in the comfort or your own home?

Festive Coffee Greetings to you all,
love Hannah xxx

How to make good coffee at home

The recipes in this book predominantly use espresso coffee so you will ideally need a coffee machine at home. The flavour of your espresso will depend on the type of machine you choose, the steam pressure it reaches, the type of coffee used and the temperature of your water. There is no right or wrong way to make your coffee: as long as you make it to your own taste, it will work in these recipes.

If you do not have a coffee machine you can use espresso instant powder. The taste will not be quite as good as a freshly brewed espresso but will still make an enjoyable hot drink.

CHOICE OF MILK

There are a wide variety of milks you can use for these recipes. I generally use skimmed dairy milk which froths very well, but whole/full-fat and semi-skimmed milks work well, and for those who do not drink dairy, there are a wide variety of plant-based milks available, such as almond, cashew, coconut and rice. These milks often come in sweetened and unsweetened versions. For the recipes in this book, it is best to use unsweetened milk as the drinks often contain syrups and so adding a sweet milk may make the drinks too sweet. The difference between latte and cappuccino is the milk to coffee ratio. In a cappuccino you should have equal quantities of espresso, steamed milk and foam, which makes a lighter coffee. Lattes traditionally have a lot more steamed milk with just a small layer of foam on top and so are a heavier drink.

STEAMING/FROTHING

There are several ways to froth milk. Many coffee machines have a milk steamer nozzle attached (pictured left), which pumps hot steam into the milk to foam it and heat it at the same time. Other machines have steam frothers, which whisk the milk with steam. If you do not have a coffee machine you can heat your milk in a saucepan on the hob/stovetop and then use an electric handheld milk frother to foam the milk in the pan. These are inexpensive and produce a really good frothy milk so are a great substitute. Both dairy and plant-based milks can be successfully frothed by using either of these methods.

COLD BREW COFFEE

Cold brew coffee is made, as its name suggests, with cold water. The coffee takes 24 hours to prepare so you need to plan ahead. It will keep for 5 days in the refrigerator but has the best taste in the first few days so it is best to make small batches more regularly rather than making a large batch, particularly as the effort involved is minimal. The general rule of thumb is that you should use 8 times the amount of water to coffee, but if you prefer a stronger coffee you can halve the amount of water. For the best flavour, I prefer to use coffee beans and grind them coarsely in a strong food processor or blender, just before making the coffee for maximum flavour, but you can use course ground coffee (suitable for a cafetiere/French press) to save time. Do not use finely ground coffee as this can lead to grounds in the coffee and give an unpleasant texture. Cold brew coffee can be used hot or cold. If serving hot, simply reheat the coffee in a saucepan. Here is a recipe:

50 g/½ cup coffee beans or coarse ground coffee
400 ml/1¾ cups water

blender or coffee grinder (if using coffee beans)
coffee filter paper or muslin

MAKES 400 ML/1¾ CUPS

Grind the beans coarsely (if using coffee beans) and place the coffee in a jug/pitcher or bowl. Pour over the cold water and cover with clingfilm/plastic wrap and leave for 24 hours to steep. You can leave in the refrigerator or at room temperature. Some say that leaving in the refrigerator can mean less coffee flavour is imparted. It is your call but I generally use the refrigerator if I am using the coffee to make cold coffees as it is ready to use at the end of steeping, rather than then having to wait longer to chill the coffee after straining. After 24 hours strain the coffee through filter paper or muslin, to remove all the coffee grounds. The strained coffee is then ready to use for your recipe of choice.

Decorating your festive drinks

There are so many ways to decorate your drinks using really simple techniques that will take your creations from ordinary to festive in a few simple flourishes.

Sprinkles – for instant wow factor use festive sugar sprinkles on top of whipped cream to add colour and a little sweetness.

Sugar crystals – sprinkle coloured sugar crystals on top of your drink which can then be stirred into the coffee to sweeten it – red and green crystals looks very Christmassy!

Candy canes – place a few peppermint candy canes in a clean plastic bag and bash with a rolling pin to crush to fine shards that can be used to decorate hot chocolates.

Edible glitter – dust the top of lattes and cappuccinos with edible glitter for a little sparkle.

Stencilling – place a festive coffee stencil on top of your drink and dust with cocoa powder, or a combination of ground sweet cinnamon mixed with sieved icing/confectioner's sugar, edible glitter or spray gold to create attractive patterns.

Feathering – drizzle a thin spiral of syrup or sauce on top of coffee foam then, using a cocktail stick, pull lines out from the centre of the spiral to the outside edge of the cup and repeat all around the cup to make a feathered pattern.

Coffee 'art' – use sauces in a piping bag to pipe festive pictures on top of your coffee such as simple holly leaves or stockings for Santa.

Basic Recipes: *Syrups & Sauces*

VANILLA SYRUP

250 ml/1 cup water
200 g/1 cup caster/granulated white sugar
1 tsp vanilla bean powder or vanilla bean paste

a sterilized jar or bottle (see page 4)

MAKES APPROX. 250 ML/1 CUP

Place all the ingredients in a saucepan and simmer over a gentle heat until the sugar has dissolved and you have a thin syrup. Store in a sterilized jar or bottle. The syrup will store for up to one month if refrigerated. Use as directed in the recipes, or as required.

GINGERBREAD SYRUP

250 ml/1 cup water
100 g/½ cup caster/white granulated sugar
100 g/½ cup brown sugar
grated zest of 1 small orange
1 tsp ground sweet cinnamon
2 cloves
½ tsp ground ginger
a pinch of freshly grated nutmeg
1 tsp vanilla bean powder or vanilla syrup
  (see above)

a sterilized jar or bottle (see page 4)

MAKES APPROX. 250 ML/1 CUP

Place all the ingredients in a saucepan and simmer over a gentle heat until the sugar has dissolved and you have a thin syrup – this should take around 5 minutes. Pass through a sieve/strainer to remove the cloves and orange zest and pour into the sterilized jar or bottle. The syrup will store for up to one month if refrigerated. Use as directed in the recipes, or as required.

PEPPERMINT SYRUP

250 ml/1 cup water
200 g/1 cup caster/white granulated sugar
2 tsp peppermint essence
½ tsp vanilla bean powder or vanilla bean paste

a sterilized jar or bottle (see page 4)

MAKES APPROX. 250 ML/1 CUP

Place all the ingredients in a saucepan and simmer over a gentle heat until the sugar has dissolved and you have a thin syrup. Store in a sterilized jar or bottle. The syrup will store for upto one month if refrigerated. Use as directed in the recipes, or as required.

CINNAMON SYRUP

250 ml/1 cup water
200 g/1 cup caster/white granulated sugar
1 tsp ground sweet cinnamon or 1 cinnamon stick

a sterilized jar or bottle (see page 4)

MAKES APPROX. 250 ML/1 CUP

Place all the ingredients in a saucepan and simmer over a gentle heat until the sugar has dissolved and you have a thin syrup. If you are using a cinnamon stick, you can leave this in the syrup, or remove before bottling, as preferred. Store in a sterilized jar or bottle. The syrup will store for up to one month if refrigerated. Use as directed in the recipes, or as required.

TOFFEE NUT SYRUP

8 chewy toffees
80 ml/⅓ cup water
80 ml/⅓ cup store-bought macadamia
  syrup, such as Monin

a sterilized jar or bottle (see page 4)

MAKES APPROX. 160 ML/⅔ CUP

*Melt the toffees in the water until
dissolved and then add the macadamia
syrup. Leave to cool and then strain
through a sieve/strainer to remove any
impurities or toffee pieces that did not
dissolve. Pour into a sterilized jar or bottle
and store in the refrigerator for up to 1 month.
Use as directed in the recipes, or as required.*

*Variations: For almond or hazelnut toffee nut
syrups, replace the macadamia syrup with a few
drops of almond extract or 2 tablespoons of either
Amaretto di Saronno or Frangelico liqueurs.*

CARAMEL SAUCE

100 g/½ cup brown sugar
40 g/3 tbsp butter
60 ml/¼ cup double/heavy cream
a pinch of salt

a sterilized jar or bottle (see page 4)

MAKES APPROX. 150 ML/⅔ CUP

*Place the brown sugar and butter in a saucepan and
stir over a gentle heat until the sugar has dissolved.
Add the cream and salt and stir to incorporate until
you have a thin caramel sauce. Leave to cool and
then pour into a sterilized jar or bottle and store for
up to one week in the refrigerator. Use as directed
in the recipes, or as required.*

CHOCOLATE SAUCE

2 tbsp light corn or golden syrup
125 ml/½ cup double/heavy cream
115 g/4 oz. dark/bittersweet chocolate
30 g/2 tbsp unsalted butter

a sterilized jar or bottle (see page 4)

MAKES APPROX. 250 ML/1 CUP

*Place all the ingredients together in a heavy-based
saucepan and whisk over a gentle heat until the
chocolate and butter have melted and the sauce
is smooth and glossy. Leave to cool and then pour
into a sterilized jar or bottle and store for up to
one week in the refrigerator. Use as directed in
the recipes, or as required.*

Vanilla latte

1–2 tbsp vanilla syrup (see page 12), to taste
1–2 shots (30–60 ml/ 1–2 oz.) freshly brewed espresso coffee
250 ml/1 cup milk of your choice
a little vanilla bean powder, to sprinkle
vanilla wafer rolls, to serve (optional)

milk steamer attachment or handheld electric milk frother

SERVES 1

Vanilla Latte is a classic and whilst it is possible to buy storebought vanilla syrups, making your own can be very satisfying and is considerably cheaper (see page 12). I love to serve this drink with filled vanilla wafer roll cookies on the side for a double vanilla hit.

Pour the vanilla syrup into the bottom of a cup or heatproof glass and pour in the hot coffee. Steam or froth the milk until very hot with a light layer of foam on top and then pour on top of the coffee. Serve at once with vanilla wafer rolls on the side, if liked.

Toffee nut latte

1–2 tbsp toffee nut syrup (see page 15), to taste
1–2 shots (30–60 ml/1–2 oz.) freshly brewed espresso coffee
250 ml/1 cup milk of your choice
whipped cream (canned is fine)
1 tsp chopped nuts
1 tsp small toffee pieces or toffee sprinkles

milk steamer attachment or handheld electric milk frother

SERVES 1

My friend Jess loves a Toffee Nut Latte more than anything! The second the syrup is available in her local coffee shop, she buys up as much as she can find so that she has enough to last her for the rest of the year (though she has usually run out by Spring!). Fear not, using my recipe on page 15 it is easy to make your own delicious version at home.

Pour the toffee nut syrup into a cup or heatproof glass and add the shots of hot coffee. Steam or froth the milk until hot and very foamy, then pour over the coffee and syrup mixture. Add a little whipped cream on top and sprinkle with chopped nuts and toffee pieces. Serve at once.

Caramel macchiato

**2 tbsp caramel sauce
(see page 15)**

**1 tbsp vanilla syrup
(see page 12)**

**1–2 shots (30–60 ml/
1–2 oz.) freshly brewed
espresso coffee**

**250 ml/1 cup milk
of your choice**

piping/pastry bag, squeezy
bottle or sundae spoon

milk steamer attachment
or handheld electric
milk frother

SERVES 1

*For a long time, this was my hot drink of choice –
strong coffee with a rich sweetness from the gooey
caramel topping. You can vary this recipe by
substituting the vanilla syrup with other flavours
that you also enjoy. I find gingerbread syrup works
particularly well during the festive holiday season.*

Prepare a heatproof glass by drizzling half of the caramel
sauce in spiral patterns inside the glass. You can do this with
a piping bag or by putting the sauce in a squeezy bottle and
using it to make distinct lines. Alternatively, you can simply
swirl in the sauce using a long-handled spoon.

Pour the vanilla syrup into the bottom of the prepared glass
and pour in the hot coffee. Steam or froth the milk until hot
there is a thin layer of foam on top and then pour over the
coffee. Drizzle the remaining caramel sauce on top of the
foam in a 'zig zag' pattern and serve at once.

Gingerbread latte

1 tbsp gingerbread syrup
(see page 12)

1–2 shots (30–60 ml/
1–2 oz.) freshly brewed
espresso coffee

250 ml/1 cup milk
of your choice

whipped cream
(canned is fine)

gingerbread cookie
crumbs, to sprinkle

mini gingerbread man,
to serve (optional)

milk steamer attachment
or handheld electric
milk frother

SERVES 1

I have my Gingerbread Latte as soon as it comes on the menu in my local coffee shop and for me that starts the countdown to the holiday season. Although you can buy many good gingerbread syrups, I love to make my own as you can vary the flavour to suit your own taste. Try my recipe on page 12 which has hints of cinnamon, cloves and orange for a typically festive flavour.

Place the gingerbread syrup into a cup or heatproof glass and add the shots of hot coffee. Steam or froth the milk until very hot with a light layer of foam on top and pour over the coffee and syrup. Add a little cream on top, sprinkle with the gingerbread cookie crumbs and add a mini gingerbread man cookie, if using. Serve at once.

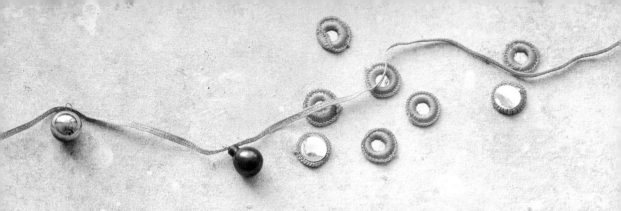

Cinnamon bun latte

100 ml/⅓ cup plus 1 tbsp
   double/heavy cream
1–2 shots (30–60 ml/
   1–2 oz.) freshly brewed
   espresso coffee
300 ml/1¼ cups milk
   of your choice
ground sweet cinnamon,
   to dust

CINNAMON BUN SYRUP
1 tbsp dark brown sugar
1 tbsp water
½ tsp ground sweet
   cinnamon
2 tsp butter

milk steamer attachment
   or handheld electric
   milk frother

SERVES 1

*I love a good cinnamon bun – the smell when
you take them out of the oven warm is utterly delicious.
This coffee is made with a syrup similar to the sticky
cinnamon bun filling and makes this drink the perfect
Christmas breakfast coffee.*

Make the cinnamon bun syrup as it needs to cool before
being whipped into the cream. Heat the brown sugar, water,
cinnamon and butter in a saucepan over a gentle heat until
you have a smooth thin syrup and the sugar has all dissolved.
Set aside to cool.

When you are ready to serve your coffee, whip the cream with
a third of the syrup until it forms soft peaks. Pour a third of
the syrup into a cup or heatproof glass and pour over the hot
coffee. Stir to incorporate the syrup into the coffee. Steam
or froth the milk until hot and foamy and pour over the coffee.
Top with the whipped cinnamon bun cream, dust with a little
cinnamon, drizzle over the remaining syrup and serve at once.

Cinnamon café bombón

60 ml/¼ cup condensed milk, or to taste

1-2 shots (30-60 ml/ 1-2 oz.) freshly brewed espresso coffee

1 tbsp whipped double/ heavy cream

a pinch of ground sweet cinnamon

SERVES 1

The café bombón is a traditional Spanish coffee, which is deliciously sweet as it's made with condensed milk. For a festive twist this is served with a little whipped cream and a sweet cinnamon dusting. Omit these two additions if you want the traditional recipe.

Pour the condensed milk into the bottom of a heatproof glass. Pour over the hot coffee, which will sit on top of the condensed milk. Place the whipped cream on top of the coffee and dust with a little cinnamon. Serve at once, swirling the coffee with a spoon before drinking to blend the coffee and condensed milk together.

Dulce de leche latte

1-2 tbsp dulce de leche sauce, plus extra to drizzle

1-2 shots (30–60 ml/ 1-2 oz.) freshly brewed espresso coffee

200 ml/¾ cup milk of your choice

50 ml/scant ¼ cup double/heavy cream, lightly whipped

silicone pastry brush

milk steamer attachment or handheld electric milk frother

SERVES 1

Dulce de leche is a caramelized milk sauce. It is made from boiling milk and sugar but luckily is readily available to buy pre-made which will save you a lot of time! I like to paint the sides of the serving glass with the caramel in swirled patterns as this looks really pretty when you fill your glass with the coffee.

Using a pastry brush, brush a tablespoonful of the dulce de leche inside a heatproof glass in swirled patterns. If you like a sweet coffee add the second tablespoon of dulce de leche to the glass, pour in the hot coffee and stir until the caramel has dissolved.

Steam or froth the milk until hot and foamy and pour over the coffee. Place a small spoonful of whipped cream on top of the coffee and drizzle with a little more dulce de leche. Serve at once.

Crème brûlée cappuccino

40 g/3¼ tbsp caster/
white granulated sugar
2–4 shots (60–120 ml)
freshly brewed
espresso coffee
500 ml/2 cups milk
of your choice
1 tsp vanilla syrup
(see page 12) or a few
drops of vanilla extract
or powder if you do
not like sweet coffee
mini marshmallows,
to decorate (optional)

silicone mat or parchment
paper
milk steamer attachment
or handheld electric
milk frother

SERVES 2

Crème brûlée is one of the most satisfying desserts I know — it makes the most delicious noise when you crack into the glazed sugar layer with a spoon. This cappuccino has a sugar decoration that melts into the drink to give a lovely burnt caramel flavour reminiscent of this popular French treat.

Begin by preparing the sugar decorations. In a dry saucepan, heat the sugar over a gentle heat until it melts and turns a golden-brown colour. It is important to keep swirling the pan so that the sugar does not burn but do not stir it. Take care towards the end as the sugar can suddenly burn quickly so remove it from the heat as soon as it is a deep golden colour. Allow to cook for 1 minute, which will allow the caramel to thicken and make better shapes. Using a spoon, swirl the hot sugar in two spiral patterns on a silicon mat or parchment paper and leave to set (which will only take a few minutes).

Pour the hot coffee into two cups or heatproof glasses. Steam or froth the milk until hot and very foamy – you want a ratio of approximately 50–50 steamed milk and foam. Add a little vanilla syrup or vanilla extract to each drink, stir, and pour the hot milk on top of the coffee. Top the drinks with marshmallows and place a sugar decoration on top of each one. Serve at once with a spoon so that you can 'crack' the topping into the coffee and stir it in.

Mountain mocha

40 g/1½ oz. milk
  chocolate Toblerone
  bar
250 ml/1 cup milk
  of your choice
1–2 shots (30–60 ml/
  1–2 oz.) freshly brewed
  espresso coffee
whipped cream
  (canned is fine)

handheld electric milk
  frother or balloon whisk

SERVES 1

Swiss Toblerone chocolate has delicious honey and almond nougat pieces in it, which infuse flavour as they melts into the milk here. Serve with a little whipped cream if you want it to be extra naughty!

Finely chop the chocolate bar and place most of it in a saucepan, reserving a little to sprinkle over your finished drink. Add the milk to the same saucepan and heat until the chocolate has melted and the milk is boiling. Use a handheld electric milk frother or balloon whisk to whisk the milk until foamy.

Pour the hot coffee into a cup or heatproof glass and add the chocolatey frothy milk. Place a little whipped cream on top of the drink, if using, sprinkle with the reserved chopped chocolate bar and serve at once.

Caramel stroopwafel latte

60 ml/¼ cup double/
heavy cream
250 ml/1 cup milk
of your choice
1–2 shots (30–60 ml/
1–2 oz.) freshly brewed
espresso coffee
1 stroopwaffle cookie,
to serve

STROOPWAFEL SAUCE

1 tbsp golden syrup/
light corn syrup
10 g/2 tsp butter
10 g/2½ tsp dark brown
sugar
½ tsp ground sweet
cinnamon

milk steamer attachment
or handheld electric
milk frother
silicone pastry brush

SERVES 1

Dutch stroopwafel cookies taste amazing. They are particularly delicious when they are placed over a hot drink for a few minutes as the steam warms the caramel filling, making it the perfect gooey texture to eat. This latte is flavoured with a delicious stroopwafel-inspired cinnamon-caramel sauce and served with a flavoured whipped cream and an actual stroopwaffle on the side to enjoy with your coffee!

Begin by preparing the stroopwafel sauce as it needs to cool before it can be added to the whipped cream. In a saucepan, heat the syrup with the butter, sugar and cinnamon until the butter and sugar have melted. Remove from the heat and let cool slightly.

In a mixing bowl, combine the cream with a large spoonful of the cooled stroopwafel sauce and whip to soft peaks.

Pour the remaining sauce into a heatproof glass and swirl into patterns in the glass using a pastry brush. Steam or froth the milk until hot and foamy. Pour the hot coffee into the prepared glass and top up with the milk until the glass is almost full. Place a spoonful of the caramel cream on top and then top with a stroopwafel cookie balanced on the edge of the glass to warm through. Serve at once, stirring the coffee so that the caramel is incorporated and enjoy the waffle once the caramel inside has softened slightly from the heat of the coffee.

Peppermint white mocha

250 ml/1 cup milk
  of your choice
50 g/1¾ oz. good-quality
  white chocolate
1 tbsp vanilla syrup
  (see page 12)
½ tsp peppermint extract
1–2 shots (30–60 ml/
  1–2 oz.) freshly brewed
  espresso coffee
candy cane stirrer,
  to serve (optional)

**DECORATED
COCOA BOMB**

10 g/⅓ oz. plain/
  bittersweet chocolate
1 mini marshmallow-filled
  store-bought milk
  chocolate cocoa bomb
1 tsp crushed candy
  canes or other festive
  peppermint candy

handheld electric milk
  frother
parchment paper or foil

SERVES 1

This drink epitomizes Christmas with a clever candy cane decorated cocoa bomb. It makes a yummy treat after a winter walk, or on Christmas Eve while waiting for Santa to arrive.

Begin by decorating the cocoa bomb. Melt the plain/bittersweet chocolate, either in a microwave for 1 minute or in a heatproof glass bowl placed over a pan of simmering water – do no let the base of the bowl touch the surface of the water. Place the bomb on a sheet of parchment paper or foil. Drizzle the melted chocolate over the bomb using a fork and sprinkle with the crushed candy cane pieces. Leave to set in the refrigerator until you are ready to serve the drink.

In a saucepan heat the milk with the white chocolate, vanilla syrup and peppermint extract and whisk with a handheld electric milk frother until the chocolate has melted and the milk is foamy. Pour the hot coffee into a cup pour over the chocolate-mint milk. Add the decorated chocolate bomb, and candy cane stirrer, if using. Serve at once and stir as the chocolate melts into the drink.

Fluffernutter latte

marshmallow fluff,
  to taste
2 tbsp honey roasted
  peanuts, finely chopped
1 tbsp smooth peanut
  butter
200 ml/¾ cup milk
  of your choice
1–2 shots (30–60 ml/
  1–2 oz.) freshly brewed
  espresso coffee

chefs' blow torch
handheld electric milk
  frother

SERVES 1

*For those of you who have not been fortunate
enough to experience it, a 'fluffernutter' is an
American sandwich with layers of peanut butter
and marshmallow fluff. It is not for the faint-
hearted as it is so very sweet, but an amazing twist
on the classic peanut butter and jelly sandwich.
This latte combines the peanut and marshmallow
elements with a caffeine hit for the perfect sugary
pick-me-up any time of day.*

First prepare a heatproof glass by dipping the top of it in
a little marshmallow fluff and then press approximately half
of the finely chopped peanuts into the fluff to decorate the
rim. Set aside.

For the peanut milk, place the peanut butter in a saucepan
with the milk and stir until the peanut butter melts into the
milk. Froth the milk with a handheld electric frother until very
foamy and the peanut butter and milk have blended together.

Pour the hot coffee into the prepared glass and top with the
frothy peanut milk. Add a large spoonful of marshmallow
fluff to the drink, then toast it with a chefs' blow torch to
caramelize the marshmallow. Sprinkle with the remaining
chopped peanuts and serve at once.

Pistachio latte

250 ml/1 cup milk
  of your choice
1 tbsp pistachio paste
  (see recipe
  introduction)
1 tbsp condensed milk
1–2 shots (30–60 ml/
  1–2 oz.) freshly brewed
  espresso coffee
1 tsp finely chopped
  pistachios, to sprinkle

whisk
handheld electric
  milk frother

SERVES 1

Pistachio perfumes this milky coffee with delicious nutty aromas. Pistachio paste is widely available in store and online but if you cannot find it you can make your own by grinding 50 g/2 oz. pistachio kernels with 1 tablespoon of flavourless oil and 1 tablespoon of icing/confectioners' sugar in a blender and blitzing until very smooth. The condensed milk makes this a very sweet drink. If you would prefer it less sweet, halve the quantity of condensed milk.

Heat the milk, pistachio paste and condensed milk in a saucepan, whisking continuously so that the pistachio paste blends with the milk. Froth the milk with a handheld electric milk frother until foamy.

Pour the hot coffee into a cup or heatproof glass and add the frothy pistachio milk. Sprinkle with chopped pistachios and serve at once.

Almond milk latte

250 ml/1 cup almond milk
1 tsp almond extract or
    1 tbsp Amaretto di
    Saronno liqueur,
    as preferred
1–2 shots (30–60 ml/
    1–2 oz.) freshly brewed
    espresso coffee
almond tuile cookies,
    to serve (optional)

handheld electric
    milk frother

SERVES 1

This almond-flavoured latte is made with almond milk so is a perfect dairy free treat. For a grown-up drink you can add a shot of Amaretto in place of the almond extract. I love to serve it with crisp almond tuile cookies on the side. I've given a cocoa bomb variation in the recipe so you can make a dairy-free almond mocha if chocolate is your thing. If you are serving to someone who has a dairy allergy, make sure that the storebought cocoa bomb you use is dairy-free (vegan versions are widely available).

Place the almond milk in a saucepan with the almond extract or Amaretto liqueur (if using) and heat until hot, then froth using a handheld electric milk frother. Pour the hot coffee into a cup or heatproof glass and pour over the foamy almond milk. Top with mini marshmallows and serve with almond cookies on the side.

COCOA BOMB VARIATION (as pictured): Place a storebought mini marshmallow filled dairy-free/vegan cocoa bomb in the cup before adding the hot almond milk. Serve at once and stir as the chocolate melts into the drink.

Toasted coconut latte

1 tbsp soft shredded coconut, to decorate

2-4 shots (60-120 ml/ 2-4 oz.) freshly brewed espresso coffee

500 ml/2 cups unsweetened coconut milk

100 ml/⅓ cup plus 1 tbsp double/heavy cream (optional)

COCONUT SYRUP

20 g/1 tbsp plus 2 tsp caster/white granulated sugar

50 g/scant ¼ cup coconut cream

handheld electric milk frother

SERVES 2

This coffee is a coconut lovers' dream made with a sweet coconut syrup that flavours both the coffee and the creamy topping. Topped with toasted coconut and made with coconut milk, this drink is coconut-tastic! If you want to make this drink suitable for anyone with a dairy intolerance, just omit the cream topping.

Make the coconut syrup first as it needs to cool before being whipped into the cream. Heat the sugar and coconut cream in a saucepan over a gentle heat until the sugar has dissolved, and you have a smooth thin syrup. Leave to cool.

Place the shredded coconut in a dry frying pan and toast until it starts to turn golden brown, stirring all the time as it can burn quickly. Once golden brown, remove from the pan and set aside until needed.

Place a spoonful of the cooled coconut syrup in two cups or heatproof glasses. Whip the cream to soft peaks with the remainder of the coconut syrup.

Pour the hot coffee into the drinks. Heat the coconut milk in a saucepan and use a handheld electric milk frother to whisk until foamy. Pour the coconut milk into each drink, top with a spoonful of coconut cream and sprinkle with the toasted coconut. Serve at once.

Pecan pie coffee

2–4 shots (60–120 ml/
2–4 oz.) freshly brewed
espresso coffee

600 m/2½ cups milk
of your choice

120 ml/½ cup double/
heavy cream

PECAN PIE SYRUP
1 tbsp dark brown sugar
½ tsp ground sweet
cinnamon
½ tsp vanilla bean paste
or powder
1 tbsp maple syrup
½ tbsp golden or light
corn syrup
10 g/2 tsp butter
20 g/scant ¼ cup pecan
halves

milk steamer attachment
or handheld electric
milk frother

SERVES 2

*Pecan pie is such a delicious dessert, and my pecan
pie syrup gives a great flavour and nutty texture to
your coffee. I enjoy having the tiny pecan pieces as an
additional texture in the coffee and to eat them at the
end with a spoon, but if you prefer you can just omit
the nuts and use the syrup for a smooth drink.*

Make the pecan pie syrup first. In a saucepan heat the sugar,
cinnamon, vanilla, both syrups, butter and 1 tablespoon
water until the sugar has melted and you have a thick syrup.
Reserve two whole pecan halves to decorate and finely chop
the remainder. Stir the chopped pecans into the syrup. You
need to use the syrup straight away as it will set as it cools.

Place a spoonful of the pecan pie syrup in the bottom of two
heatproof glasses or cups and swirl the glasses so that the
syrup coats the inside, then pour in the hot coffee. Steam or
froth the milk until hot and foamy and pour into the glasses
or cups. Whip the cream to soft peaks and place a spoonful
on top of each drink. Top with the reserved pecan halves and
drizzle over the remaining pecan pie syrup. Serve at once.

Millionaire's pretzel latte

1 tbsp caramel sauce (see page 15), plus extra to drizzle

60 ml/¼ cup double/heavy cream

1 tbsp chocolate sauce (see page 15), plus extra to drizzle

1–2 shots (30–60 ml/1–2 oz.) freshly brewed espresso coffee

250 ml/1 cup milk of your choice

2 milk chocolate-coated salted pretzels

cocoa powder, to dust

piping/pastry bag, squeezy bottle or sundae spoon

milk steamer attachment or handheld electric milk frother

SERVES 1

This recipe combines two things I love – millionaire's shortbread and pretzels. Topped with a chocolate cream, caramel swirls and chocolate-coated pretzels in place of the shortbread for pleasing crunch, this is a highly indulgent coffee-time treat.

Prepare a heatproof glass by drizzling the caramel sauce in spiral patterns inside the glass. You can do this with a piping bag or by putting the sauce in a squeezy bottle and using it to make distinct lines. Alternatively, you can simply swirl in the sauce using a long-handled sundae spoon.

In a mixing bowl whip the cream and chocolate sauce together until soft peaks form. Set aside.

Pour the hot coffee into the prepared glass. Steam or froth the milk until hot and foamy and then pour into the glass. Top the drink with the chocolate cream and drizzle over some caramel sauce and chocolate sauce. Add the pretzels and dust with a little cocoa powder. Serve at once.

Chai latte

1 chai tea bag

300 ml/1¼ cups milk of your choice

1 tbsp gingerbread syrup (see page 12) or 1 tbsp vanilla syrup (see page 12) or honey

1 tbsp mini marshmallows (optional)

ground sweet cinnamon, to dust

1 star anise, to garnish (optional)

milk steamer attachment or handheld electric milk frother

SERVES 1

This is a tea-based latte gently spiced with warming cinnamon and cardamon. If you do not have syrups to hand you can just sweeten the drink with honey. I've included a cocoa bomb variation here for an indulgent chocolate drink. (Tip: If you are using star anise to garnish your drink as shown, remove it before serving as it should not be eaten.)

Place the chai tea bag in a saucepan with the milk and gingerbread or vanilla syrup and heat until the milk is hot. Remove the teabag and then use a handheld electric frother to foam the milk. Pour into a heatproof glass, top with a few marshmallows, if using, dust with a little cinnamon, add a star anise to garnish and serve at once.

COCOA BOMB VARIATION (as pictured): Omit the marshmallows listed and place a storebought mini marshmallow filled cocoa bomb in the cup before adding the hot chai. Serve at once and stir as the chocolate melts into the drink.

Matcha latte

1 tbsp matcha green tea
powder, plus extra
to dust
250 ml/1 cup milk
of your choice
50 g/2 oz. good-quality
white chocolate
1 tbsp mini marshmallows

matcha whisk, or similar

SERVES 1

*I have been lucky enough to make several trips to the
wonderful Barakura English Garden in Japan in recent
years. On every trip I have enjoyed the delights of
delicious matcha green tea – whisked perfectly with
bamboo whisks. This recipe is inspired by those tea
houses and their delicious tea. Matcha can be an
acquired taste as it has a bitter flavour but it is
tempered here by the sweetness of white chocolate.*

Place the matcha tea powder in a bowl with 1 tablespoon
hot water and whisk until the matcha powder has blended
with the water. Add the matcha and water mixture to a
saucepan with the milk and white chocolate and heat over
a gentle heat until the chocolate has melted. Whisk again
vigorously to ensure all the matcha powder is incorporated
and you have no lumps. Pour the hot matcha milk into a
heatproof glass, top with mini marshmallows and dust with
a little matcha powder. Serve at once.

COCOA BOMB VARIATION (as pictured): Omit the white
chocolate and marshmallows listed and place a storebought
mini marshmallow filled white cocoa bomb in the cup before
adding the hot matcha milk. Serve at once and stir as the
chocolate melts into the drink.

Rum coffee with burnt sugar syrup & chocolate coffee beans

400 ml/1¾ cups milk
  of your choice
30 ml/2 tbsp spiced rum
2–4 shots (60–120 ml/
  1–2 oz.) freshly brewed
  espresso coffee
chocolate-covered coffee
  beans, to garnish

BURNT SUGAR SYRUP
30 g/2½ tbsp caster/
  white granulated sugar
20 g/1 tbsp dark brown
  sugar

handheld electric milk
  frother

SERVES 2

This is a cappuccino with the irresistible addition of rum so it is great for serving as an after-dinner treat. You can substitute the rum with other spirits of your choice — such as Amaretto di Saronno and Tia Maria.

Make the burnt sugar syrup first. In a dry saucepan heat the both the sugars over a gentle heat until the sugar melts and turns a dark brown colour. It is important to keep moving and swirling the pan so that the sugar does not burn but do not stir it. Take care towards the end as the sugar can suddenly burn quickly so remove it as soon as it is a deep golden colour. When the sugar is dark golden brown add 2 tablespoons water to the pan and stir until the sugar has dissolved and you have a thin syrup. Set aside.

Heat the milk and spiced rum in a saucepan and use a handheld electric frother to whisk until foamy. Pour the hot coffee into two cups or heatproof glasses and top with the foamed rum milk. Drizzle with the burnt sugar syrup and top with chocolate-covered coffee beans. Serve at once.

COCOA BOMB VARIATION (as pictured): Place a storebought mini marshmallow filled white cocoa bomb in each cup before adding the hot rum milk. Add chocolate-covered coffee beans to garnish. Serve at once and stir as the chocolate melts into the drink.

Caribbean cafe with rum & Malibu

2–4 tsp brown sugar, to taste

2 tbsp dark rum

2 tbsp Malibu or other coconut-flavoured rum

250 ml/1 cup freshly brewed cafetière/ French press or filter coffee

80 ml/⅓ cup whipping cream

balloon whisk

flat-bottomed barspoon or teaspoon

SERVES 2

This flavoured coffee is similar to an Irish coffee where the alcohol and coffee are combined in a glass, then lightly whipped cream is carefully poured on top over the back of a spoon so it floats on the surface. Traditionally you then drink the coffee through the layer of frothy cream.

Divide the sugar, both rums and hot coffee between two heatproof glasses and stir well.

Put the cream in a bowl and whisk until foaming. Slowly layer the cream over the surface of each coffee, using a flat-bottomed barspoon or a teaspoon. Serve at once.

Egg-nog latte

500 ml/2 cups milk
of your choice
1 vanilla pod/bean, split
2 very fresh eggs
2–3 tbsp brown sugar,
to taste
½ teaspoon ground
sweet cinnamon
a pinch of grated nutmeg,
plus extra to dust
2 tbsp dark rum
250 ml/1 cup freshly
brewed cafetiere/
French press or filter
coffee

balloon whisk

SERVES 4

*This warming, festive drink with a hint of coffee
makes a lovely alternative to the more traditional
egg nog. For a non-alcoholic version, omit the rum.*

Put the milk and vanilla pod/bean in a saucepan and heat
gently until the milk just reaches boiling point.

Meanwhile, put the eggs, sugar and spices in a bowl and
whisk until frothy. Stir in the milk, then return the mixture to
the pan. Heat gently for 2–3 minutes, stirring constantly with
a wooden spoon, until the mixture thickens slightly.

Remove from the heat and stir in the rum and coffee. Discard
the vanilla pod/bean. Pour into four cups or heatproof
glasses, dust with a little grated nutmeg and serve at once.

Pumpkin latte

375 ml/1½ cups milk of your choice

100 g/3½ oz. cooked sweet pumpkin, mashed, or canned pumpkin purée

3 tbsp brown sugar (omit if using canned purée)

¼ tsp ground sweet cinnamon

250 ml/1 cup freshly brewed cafetière/French press or filter coffee

whipped cream (canned is fine) and cinnamon sugar, to serve

balloon whisk

SERVES 4

Perfect for any wintertime party, this thick, richly spiced latte is flavoured with sweetened pumpkin. If you can find canned sweetened pumpkin purée, then use this and omit the sugar in the recipe.

Put the milk, pumpkin, sugar (if using) and cinnamon in a saucepan and heat gently, whisking constantly until the mixture just reaches boiling point. Transfer to four cups or heatproof glasses and stir in the coffee.

Top with whipped cream and a dusting of cinnamon sugar. Serve at once.

Mochas & hot chocolates

Snowmallow white chocolate mocha

500 ml/2 cups milk
  of your choice
80 g/2¾ oz. good-quality
  white chocolate
½ tsp vanilla bean
  powder or paste
2–4 shots (60–120 ml/
  2–4 oz.) freshly brewed
  espresso coffee

TO DECORATE
a few drops of orange
  food colouring gel
10 g/⅓ oz. good-quality
  white chocolate, melted
2 giant marshmallows
10 g/⅓ oz. dark/
  bittersweet chocolate,
  melted

cocktail stick/toothpick
balloon whisk

SERVES 2

This is a light and creamy mocha with the sweetness of white chocolate and a strong hit of espresso. To make it super festive float these cute snowmen marshmallows on top of your mocha. If you can't find giant marshmallows, you can use smaller marshmallows and have a 'melt' of snowmen on top of your drink.

Make the marshmallow snowmen to give the chocolate time to set. Mix a few drops of the orange food colouring gel into the melted white chocolate so that you have an even orange colour. Use a cocktail stick to place two dots of the dark chocolate for eyes and five dots for a mouth on each of the giant marshmallows. Using a second clean cocktail stick use the orange chocolate to draw on noses in the shapes of carrots.

Heat the milk in a saucepan and add the white chocolate and vanilla. Whisk as the chocolate melts to blend it with the milk. Pour the hot coffee into two cups or heatproof glasses and pour over the hot white mocha. Float a snowman marshmallow on top of each cup and serve at once.

Hazelnut mocha

100 g/3½ oz. milk/semi-
sweet chocolate, chopped

500 ml/2 cups milk
of your choice

2 shots (60 ml/2 oz.) freshly
brewed espresso coffee

1 heaped tbsp chocolate
hazelnut spread
(suchas Nutella)

4–6 tbsp Frangelico liqueur
(optional)

200 ml/generous ¾ cup
double/heavy cream

1 tbsp finely toasted
chopped hazelnuts

balloon whisk

SERVES 2

This drink is a must for all hazelnut lovers – rich and creamy with a hint of optional hazelnut-flavoured liqueur. Finished with fluffy whipped cream and sprinkled with crunchy toasted hazelnuts, this is an utterly nutterly treat!

Place the chopped chocolate in a heatproof bowl set over a pan of simmering water and heat gently over a low heat until melted – do not let the base of the bowl touch the surface of the water.

Place the milk in a saucepan and bring gently to the boil. Add the melted chocolate, coffee and chocolate hazelnut spread to the pan and simmer over low heat, whisking all the time, until the chocolate is combined. Remove from the heat and add the hazelnut liqueur to taste, if using. Pour the drink into two cups or heatproof glasses.

Whip the cream to stiff peaks and add a spoonful to the top of each drink. Sprinkle with toasted hazelnuts. Serve at once.

S'mores hot chocolate

100 g/3½ oz. milk/
  semi-sweet chocolate,
  chopped
2 graham crackers or
  digestive biscuits,
  crushed with a rolling
  pin into crumbs
250 ml/1 cup milk
  of your choice
250 ml/1 cup double/
  heavy cream
2 giant marshmallows

balloon whisk
chef's blow torch

SERVES 2

S'mores are a delicious campside treat popular all over America — toasted marshmallows and chocolate are sandwiched between graham crackers or digestive biscuits. That delicious combination is the inspiration for this fun and warming drink. You will need a chef's blow torch for this recipe.

Preparing two heatproof glasses first. Place the chopped chocolate in a heatproof bowl set over a pan of simmering water and heat over a low heat until melted – do not let the base of the bowl touch the surface of the water. Carefully dip the rims of each glass into the chocolate.

Place the cracker/biscuit crumbs on a plate and dip the chocolate-coated rim of each glass in the crumbs to coat. Set aside until you are ready to serve.

Spoon the remaining melted chocolate into a saucepan with the milk and cream, and heat over low heat, whisking all the time. Pour the hot chocolate into the prepared glasses, taking care not to pour over the chocolate-crumb rim decoration.

Place each marshmallow on a fork and toast with the blow torch to caramelize. Take care not to burn the marshmallows. While the marshmallows are still warm, place one on top of each drink. Serve at once.

Chai-spiced white hot chocolate

12 green cardamom pods
1 tsp caster/white
  granulated sugar
1 cinnamon stick
a pinch of freshly grated
  nutmeg, plus extra
  to dust
500 ml/2 cups milk
  of your choice
1 tsp rose extract or rose
  syrup
100 g/3½ oz. good-
  quality white chocolate,
  chopped

pestle and mortar or spice
  grinder
balloon whisk

SERVES 2

Chai tea is a popular hot drink in India, delicately fragranced with cinnamon and cardamom. The spicing of the tea varies from region to region, and every family's recipe for the chai masala is different. I have used that delicious drink as the inspiration for this white hot chocolate with warming spices and just a hint of rose water for added perfume. For a refreshing alternative, you can also serve this chilled and poured over ice.

Begin by removing the black seeds from two of the cardamom pods and grinding them to a fine powder with the sugar using a pestle and mortar or a spice grinder.

Place the ground cardamom and remaining pods in a saucepan with the cinnamon stick, nutmeg and milk, and bring to the boil over a low heat. Remove from the heat and leave the spices to infuse for 15–20 minutes, then discard the whole pods and cinnamon stick.

Add the rose extract and chopped white chocolate to the pan and return to a simmer over low heat, whisking all the time, until the chocolate has melted. Pour into two cups or heatproof glasses and dust with freshly grated nutmeg. Serve at once.

Mocha maple coffee

500 ml/2 cups freshly
brewed cafetière/
French press or filter
coffee
2 shots (60 ml/2 oz.)
crème de cacao
125 ml/½ cup whipping
cream
1 tsp maple syrup
roughly grated dark/
bittersweet chocolate,
to sprinkle

balloon whisk
flat-bottomed barspoon
or teaspoon

SERVES 2

Coffee and chocolate make perfect partners, as this delicious drink proves. The addition of sweet, maple-flavoured cream makes this an indulgent treat and the perfect after-dinner drink.

Pour the hot coffee into two heatproof glasses or cups and add a shot of crème de cacao to each one.

Lightly whisk the cream and maple syrup together until the mixture is foaming and thickened slightly. Slowly layer the cream over the surface of the coffee using a flat-bottomed barspoon or a teaspoon. Sprinkle with grated chocolate and serve at once.

Malted hot chocolate

100 g/3½ oz. milk/
   semi-sweet chocolate,
   chopped

250 ml/1 cup milk
   of your choice

450 ml/1¾ cups double/
   heavy cream

3 tbsp malted drink
   powder (such as
   Horlicks or Ovaltine)

chocolate-coated malt
   balls (such as Maltesers
   or Whoppers),
   chopped

balloon whisk

SERVES 2

Malted drinks are among the most comforting and this hot chocolate is what I drink when I am in need of a hug in a mug! Top with whipped cream and chocolate-coated malt balls for an extra special treat.

Place the chopped chocolate in a heatproof bowl set over a pan of simmering water and heat gently over low heat until melted – do not let the base of the bowl touch the surface of the water.

Place the milk and 250 ml/1 cup of the cream in a saucepan and gently bring to the boil. Add the melted chocolate to the pan with the malted drink powder and simmer over low heat until the chocolate is combined, whisking all the time. Pour the hot chocolate into two cups or heatproof glasses.

Whip the remaining cream to stiff peaks and place a large spoonful on top of each drink. Sprinkle with the crushed malt balls and serve at once.

Peppermint candy cane hot chocolate

50 g/2 oz. good-quality
  white chocolate,
  chopped
3 candy canes, 1 crushed
  in a plastic bag with
  a rolling pin
100 g/3½ oz. chocolate-
  coated mint fondants
  (such as After Eights)
250 ml/1 cup milk
  of your choice
450 ml/scant 2 cups
  double/heavy cream

balloon whisk

SERVES 2

Candy canes make the perfect stirrer for this festive hot chocolate. To make your glasses extra special, dip the rims in melted white chocolate and crushed candy canes. This drink is made with chocolate-coated mint fondants such as After Eights, although you could substitute peppermint-flavoured dark/bittersweet chocolate, if you prefer. For a white chocolate variation, use white chocolate and a teaspoon of peppermint extract or white chocolate-coated mint fondants, if you can find them.

Start by preparing the glasses. Place the white chocolate in a heatproof bowl over a pan of simmering water and heat until melted – do not let the base of the bowl touch the surface of the water.

Carefully dip the rims of two heatproof glasses or cups into the chocolate. Place the crushed candy cane pieces on a plate and roll the edge of the rim of each chocolate-coated glass in them to decorate. Set aside, reserving any leftover to sprinkle over the drink.

Place the chocolate-coated mint fondants in a saucepan with the milk and 250 ml/1 cup of the cream and bring to the boil over a low heat, whisking all the time. Pour the hot chocolate into the prepared glasses, taking care not to pour it over the decorated rims.

Whip the remaining cream to stiff peaks and place a large spoonful on top of each drink. Sprinkle with any leftover candy cane pieces and place a candy cane in each glass to serve. Serve at once.

Terry's chocolate orange hot chocolate

250 ml/1 cup milk of your choice

50 g/2 oz. Terry's chocolate orange, plus extra 'segments' to serve

whipped cream (canned is fine)

finely grated orange zest

handheld electric milk frother or balloon whisk

SERVES 1

Every festive season there is always a Terry's chocolate orange in our stockings from Santa so this drink instantly transports me to Christmas day mornings. If you cannot find a Terry's Chocolate Orange easily substitute any plain/bittersweet chocolate-orange bar.

Place the milk in a saucepan with the 50 g/2 oz. chocolate orange and simmer until melted, stirring all the time. Once the milk is hot, remove from the heat and froth with a handheld electric milk frother or whisk until all the chocolate is blended with the milk and the hot chocolate is very frothy.

Pour into a cup or heatproof glass and top with the whipped cream. Sprinkle over a little orange zest and decorate with 'segments' of chocolate orange. Serve at once.

Turkish delight hot chocolate

100 g/3½ oz. dark/
bittersweet chocolate,
chopped

350 ml/1½ cups milk
of your choice

350 ml/1½ cups double/
heavy cream

1 tbsp caster/white
granulated sugar

2 tsp storebought rose
syrup

4 cubes mixed pink
and red Turkish delight
candy

balloon whisk

piping/pastry bag fitted
with a large star
nozzle/tip (optional)

SERVES 2

*This hot chocolate hints at the flavours of the
Levantine with fragrant rose. Topped with cubed
Turkish delight candy, this is a drink to serve to
people you love. It is rich and indulgent, made with
dark/bittersweet chocolate, so sweeten with sugar
or honey to suit your taste.*

Place the chopped chocolate in a saucepan with the
milk, 150 ml/⅔ cup of the cream, the sugar and 1 teaspoon
of the rose syrup. Heat gently over a low heat until the
chocolate and sugar have melted, whisking all the time.
Remove the hot chocolate from the heat while you prepare
the cream topping.

Place the remaining cream in a bowl with the final teaspoon
of rose syrup and whisk to stiff peaks. Spoon the cream
into the piping/pastry bag, if using. (Alternatively you can
use a spoon to swirl the cream on top of the drink.)

Gently reheat the hot chocolate if necessary and pour
into cups or heatproof glasses. Pipe or spoon a swirl of
whipped cream on top of each glass. Finely chopped
the Turkish delight and sprinkle over the drink.
Serve at once.

Toffee apple hot chocolate

1 red dessert apple

freshly squeezed juice of ½ lemon

1 tsp ground sweet cinnamon

100 g/½ cup caster/ superfine sugar

500 ml/2 cups milk of your choice

40 g/1½ oz. good-quality white chocolate, chopped

4 tbsp Apfelkorn liqueur (optional)

whipped cream (canned is fine)

caramel sauce (see page 15) or dulce de leche, to drizzle

mandoline (optional

silicone mat or baking sheet lined with parchment paper

balloon whisk

SERVES 2

Biting into the crisp caramel shell of a toffee apple to find the juicy apple underneath is one of life's simple pleasures. This drink is flavoured with caramelized sugar, and you should take the caramel as dark as you dare (without burning it) to get the deepest caramel flavour into the milk. The optional Apfelkorn liqueur is a tasty German apple spirit which is VERY warming!

Preheat the oven to 140°C (275°F) Gas 1.

Leaving the skin on, cut the apple into thin slices using a mandoline or a sharp knife. Toss the slices in lemon juice to prevent them browning, then dust in a little cinnamon. Lay the slices out flat on a baking sheet and place in the preheated oven for 1–1½ hours, until dried but still slightly soft. (This will make more dried apple than you need for decoration but they will keep well and make a great healthy snack if stored in an airtight container.)

Place the sugar in a saucepan and heat gently over a low heat until melted. Do not stir, but swirl it to ensure that the sugar does not burn. Once the sugar has melted, carefully dip some of the baked apple slices into the caramel – only dipping them in half way. (Use tongs and take extreme care as the sugar is very hot and can burn you.) Place the apple slices on a silicon mat or lined baking sheet and leave to dry.

Add the milk to the remaining caramelized sugar in the pan. Do not worry if the sugar solidifies, as it will melt on heating. Simmer over low heat until the sugar dissolves. Add the chocolate and stir until melted. Remove from the heat and add the Apfelkorn, if using (do not return the mixture to the heat as it may curdle the milk). Pour the hot chocolate into two cups or heatproof glasses, top with a little whipped cream and drizzle with caramel sauce or dulce de leche. Place an apple slice on top of each cup. Serve at once.

Red velvet hot chocolate

500 ml/2 cups milk
  of your choice
100 g/3½ oz. milk/
  semi-sweet chocolate,
  chopped
1 tbsp unsweetened
  cocoa powder, sifted
a few drops of red food
  colouring
2 scoops of vanilla
  ice cream
red velvet cake crumbs
  or sugar sprinkles,
  to decorate

balloon whisk
ice cream scoop
sundae spoons

SERVES 2

This hot chocolate is inspired by the ever-popular red velvet cake, which is traditionally made with cocoa powder and red food colouring. The same ingredients are used in this hot chocolate and, for extra fun, each serving is topped with a scoop of ice cream so you can enjoy the hot/cold sensation as you drink this treat. If you are serving this with a slice of red velvet cake, sprinkle a few crumbs on top. If you don't have a red velvet cake to hand, use some sugar sprinkles instead.

Place the milk and chopped chocolate in a saucepan with the cocoa powder and simmer over a low heat until the chocolate has melted and the cocoa is incorporated, whisking constantly.

Add a few drops of red food colouring to give the drink the trademark 'red velvet' dark reddish brown colour.

Pour the hot chocolate into two cups or heatproof glasses, place a scoop of ice cream on top of each and decorate with cake crumbs or sugar sprinkles. Serve at once with sundae spoons to eat the ice cream.

Gingerbread-spiced hot chocolate

100 g/3½ oz. milk/
  semi-sweet chocolate,
  chopped
500 ml/2 cups milk
  of your choice
1 ball preserved stem
  ginger and 1 tbsp ginger
  syrup from the jar
1 tbsp gingerbread syrup
  (see page 12)
whipped cream
  (canned is fine)
gingerbread man
  sprinkles, to decorate

balloon whisk

SERVES 2

I love the flavour of ginger, and gingerbread hot chocolate is one of my all-time favourites. You can make this drink with milk/semi-sweet, dark/bittersweet or white chocolate and they are all equally delicious. Flavoured with stem ginger and gingerbread syrup, this is the perfect drink to sip by the fireside. For an extra treat, serve with gingerbread cookies on the side. If you do not have time to make a gingerbread syrup, simply double the quantity of ginger syrup you use from the stem ginger jar and add a little ground cinnamon and a pinch of grated nutmeg to the milk.

Place the chopped chocolate in a saucepan with the milk, stem ginger, stem ginger syrup and gingerbread syrup. Simmer over a low heat until the chocolate has melted, whisking all the time.

Remove the stem ginger and discard. Pour the hot chocolate into two cups or heatproof glasses, top with whipped cream and gingerbread man sprinkles. Serve at once.

Chocolate brownie mega hot chocolate

50 ml/2 oz. double/
  heavy cream
1 tbsp golden/light corn
  syrup
1 tbsp cocoa powder
1 tbsp brown sugar
½ tsp vanilla extract
  or vanilla bean paste
50 g/2 oz. dark/
  bittersweet chocolate,
  chopped
1 tbsp melted butter
400 ml/1¾ cups milk
  of your choice

TO SERVE
100 ml/3⅓ oz. double/
  heavy cream
2 tbsp marshmallow fluff
mini marshmallows
1 tsp finely grated dark/
  bittersweet chocolate
1 chocolate brownie,
  cut into small pieces

a handheld electric milk
  frother or balloon whisk

SERVES 2

Brownies and hot chocolate are the perfect way to spend a winter evening – this hot chocolate is rich with all the flavours of a brownie with cocoa and brown sugar and the drink is finished off with whipped marshmallow cream, grated chocolate and brownie pieces. This is probably the most indulgent hot chocolate in this book – enjoy!

In a saucepan, heat the cream with the syrup, cocoa powder, brown sugar and vanilla. Once the sugar has dissolved add the chopped chocolate and butter and simmer until the chocolate is melted, stirring constantly. Add the milk and stir until the chocolate sauce is incorporated into the milk. Froth with a handheld electric milk frother or whisk until the chocolate milk is foamy.

In a bowl, whisk together the cream and marshmallow fluff until the mixture holds soft peaks. Pour the hot chocolate into two cups or heatproof glasses and top with the marshmallow cream, some mini marshmallows, grated chocolate and a few small brownie pieces. Serve at once.

Coconut hot chocolate

1 tbsp shredded coconut

100 g/3½ oz. milk/semi-sweet chocolate, chopped

250 ml/1 cup milk of your choice

250 ml/1 cup double/heavy cream

160 ml/scant ⅔ cup coconut cream

5 tbsp coconut rum, such as Malibu (optional)

double/heavy cream, whipped to stiff peaks, to top

balloon whisk

SERVES 2

This delicious hot chocolate is laced with rum and coconut cream — perfect for a taste of Caribbean sunshine when it's chilly outside. I like to add a little toasted shredded coconut on top for decoration and texture. (Tip: Omit the rum to serve to children.)

Start by toasting the coconut in a dry frying pan/skillet, stirring all the time until it is golden brown. Take care as the coconut can burn easily. As soon as it starts to turn lightly golden brown, tip it out onto a plate to cool.

Place the chopped chocolate in a heatproof bowl set over a pan of simmering water and heat gently until melted – do not let the base of the bowl touch the surface of the water.

Spoon the melted chocolate into a saucepan with the milk, cream and coconut cream and bring gently to the boil, whisking all the time. Remove from the heat and add the coconut rum.

Pour the hot chocolate into two cups or heatproof glasses. Top with whipped cream and the toasted coconut. Serve at once.

Irish dream

100 g/3½ oz. good-
quality white chocolate
(you will need a bar
to grate the flakes
for decoration)

450 ml/scant 2 cups
double/heavy cream

250 ml/1 cup milk
of your choice

100 ml/⅓ cup Baileys,
or other Irish cream
liqueur

1 tbsp caramel sauce
(see page 15), plus
extra to drizzle

box grater
balloon whisk

SERVES 2

*When it is cold, Irish cream liqueurs are perfect for
warming the soul, and what better way to do this than
by flavouring hot chocolate with this delicious whiskey-
based drink. This rich and luxurious hot chocolate
is topped with whipped caramel cream and curls of
white chocolate, making it one very indulgent tipple!*

Start by making the white chocolate flakes. Grate the bar on
a box grater to create generous flakes. (It is best to do this
with the chocolate at room temperature rather than chilled,
so that it doesn't break.) Put the chocolate flakes on a small
plate and keep in the refrigerator until you are ready to serve.

Chop the remaining white chocolate into chunks and place
in a saucepan with 250 ml/1 cup of the cream and the milk.
Simmer over a low heat until the chocolate has melted,
whisking all the time. Remove from the heat and add the
Baileys or cream liqueur.

Place the remaining cream in a mixing bowl with the caramel
sauce and whisk to stiff peaks. Pour the hot chocolate into
two cups or heatproof glasses and spoon some caramel
cream on top. Drizzle with a little extra caramel sauce, if
liked, and top with the chocolate flakes. Serve at once.

Maple-pecan bourbon hot chocolate

100 g/3½ oz. milk/
   semi-sweet chocolate,
   chopped
250 ml/1 cup double/
   heavy cream
250 ml/1 cup milk
   of your choice
100 ml/⅓ cup maple
   syrup
1 tsp vanilla bean paste
   or pure vanilla extract
100 ml/⅓ cup bourbon
   whiskey

PECAN PRALINE
50 g/¼ cup caster/
   superfine sugar
3 tbsp pecan halves

silicone mat or greased
   baking sheet
blender
balloon whisk

SERVES 2

This is proper grown-up hot chocolate — manly hot chocolate if you will! Laced with bourbon whiskey and maple syrup it warms you to the core. It's a great drink for adults to take out in a flask for cold winter walks or watching sports fixtures.

Make the pecan praline first. Heat the sugar in a saucepan until it melts, swirling the pan constantly. Do not stir with a spoon. Watch it carefully as it can burn very easily. Once the sugar is a golden caramel colour, spread the pecans out on a silicone mat or greased baking sheet, and then pour over the caramel. Leave to cool, then blitz to fine crumbs in a blender. Place the praline powder on a plate.

Next prepare two cups or heatproof glasses. Place the chopped chocolate in a heatproof bowl set over a pan of simmering water until melted – do not let the base of the bowl touch the surface of the water. Carefully dip the rim of each glass or cup into the melted chocolate then, roll the rim of each chocolate-rimmed glass in the praline powder. Set aside until ready to serve.

Spoon the remaining melted chocolate into a saucepan and add the cream, milk, maple syrup, vanilla and bourbon. Simmer over a low heat until combined, whisking all the time. Pour the hot chocolate into the prepared glasses, taking care not to pour it over the decorated rims. Serve at once.

Cherry brandy hot chocolate

6 Maraschino cherries

100 g/3½ oz. dark/
   bittersweet chocolate,
   chopped

1 tbsp icing/
   confectioners' sugar

250 ml/1 cup milk
   of your choice

250 ml/1 cup double/
   heavy cream

5 tbsp cherry brandy

2 tbsp canned red or
   black cherry pie filling

whipped cream, to serve
   (optional)

2 wooden skewers, about
   5 cm 2 in. taller than
   your serving glasses

balloon whisk

2 sundae spoons

SERVES 2

This is a delicious hot chocolate drink with a grown-up kick. It is indulgent and warming with a splash of cherry brandy, a cute little maraschino cherry stick, which adds a touch of festive reindeer nose red to the presentation! Serve with whipped cream on the side.

Thread the cherries onto the wooden skewers and set aside.

Place the chopped chocolate In a saucepan with the sugar, milk and double/heavy cream. Simmer over low heat until the chocolate has melted, whisking all the time. Remove from the heat and add the cherry brandy.

Place a tablespoonful of cherry pie filling into the bottom of two heatproof glasses or cups, then carefully pour in the hot chocolate milk.

Place a cherry skewer in each glass. Serve at once with a small bowl of whipped cream on the side, if liked, ready to spoon into the drink. Have sundae spoons ready to enjoy the warm cherry pie filling at the bottom of the glass.

Frappés, shakes & cold brews

Iced toffee nut frappé

1–2 shots (30–60 ml/
   1–2 oz.) freshly brewed
   espresso coffee, cooled
200 ml/³⁄₄ cup milk
   of your choice
2 tbsp toffee nut syrup
   (see page 15)
a handful of crushed ice
60 ml/¹⁄₄ cup double/
   heavy cream
a spoonful of chopped
   toasted macadamia
   nuts
caramel sauce
   (see page 15),
   to drizzle (optional)

blender
balloon whisk
piping/pastry bag
   (optional)
paper drinking straws

SERVES 1

Frappés are thick, ice-blended drinks that can be prepared in a blender — make sure you use lots of ice for a proper slushie effect. This is a frozen version of the popular toffee nut latte (see page 20). It is topped with a tempting toffee-nut cream and toasted nuts.

Place the cooled coffee, milk, 1 tablespoon of the toffee nut syrup and ice in a blender and blitz until all the ice is blended and you have a thick slushie mixture.

Place the cream in a bowl with the remaining 1 tablespoon toffee nut syrup and whisk until you have very soft peaks. Spoon into a piping bag, if using.

Pour the frappé into a tall glass and pipe (or spoon) the toffee nut whipped cream on top. Top with the chopped nuts and a little drizzle of caramel sauce, if using. Serve at once with drinking straws.

Gingerbread cold brew iced latte

100 ml/3⅓ oz. cold brew
coffee (see page 9)
2 tbsp gingerbread syrup
(see page 12)
200 ml/¾ cup milk
of your choice
a handful of crushed ice
60 ml/¼ cup double/
heavy cream
gingerbread crumbs
candied orange peel
mini gingerbread man
cookies, to serve
(optional)

blender
balloon whisk
paper drinking straws

SERVES 1

This iced festive milky coffee is a perfect treat – the homemade gingerbread syrup has hints of orange, cloves, cinnamon and vanilla and will remind you of the smell of gingerbread baking in the oven.

Place the coffee, 1 tablespoon of gingerbread syrup, milk and ice in a blender and blitz well. Pour into a tall glass, top up the with cold milk until it is almost full, leaving room for the whipped cream topping.

Place the cream in a bowl, add the remaining 1 tablespoon gingerbread syrup and whisk to soft peaks. Spoon the gingerbread whipped cream on top of the drink.

Sprinkle over the gingerbread crumbs and candied orange peel. Add a mini gingerbread man cookie, if using. Serve at once with drinking straws.

'Cereal milk' shake

50 g/⅓ cup marshmallow cereal (such as Lucky Charms or Marshmallow Mateys), plus extra to decorate

250 ml/1 cup milk of your choice

5 scoops vanilla ice cream

1 tbsp whipped cream (canned is fine)

1 tbsp marshmallow fluff

blender
paper drinking straws

SERVES 1

When I visit my brother in New York we often go to the Milk Bar, the amazing cake shop run by Christina Tosi. I am always intrigued by their bottles of cereal milk drinks, which are flavoured by adding cereal and leaving it to soak and infuse the milk. This is my inspiration for this fun retro shake. Made with Lucky Charms or Marshmallow Mateys, it may transport you back to your childhood!

Place the cereal and milk in a bowl and leave in the refrigerator for 1 hour. Strain the milk into the blender through a fine mesh sieve/strainer and discard the soggy cereal.

Add 4 scoops of the ice cream to the blender and blitz until the shake is smooth and all the ice cream is blended into the milk. Pour into a tall glass and top with the remaining scoop of ice cream, the whipped or canned cream, marshmallow fluff and sprinkle with more marshmallow cereal. Serve at once with drinking straws.

Spiced iced frappé

1 tbsp good-quality
  instant espresso
  powder
1 tbsp hot water
200 ml/¾ cup
  evaporated milk
1 tbsp gingerbread syrup
  or cinnamon syrup
  (see page 12)
a large handful of
  crushed ice or ice
  cubes, as preferred

blender
paper drinking straws

SERVES 1

*In Greece 'frappé' is everywhere and is made by shaking
chilled milk and instant coffee in a lidded container
to create a smooth foamy head when is then poured
over ice. Drinking them always reminds me of holidays
under the hot summer sun. Adding a little cinnamon
syrup gives this pick-me-up drink a little festive twist.*

Dissolve the espresso powder in the hot water, then place all
the ingredients in a blender and blitz for a few minutes until
the coffee is an icy slushie.

Taste for sweetness, adding a little more sugar or syrup if you
prefer a sweeter drink. Pour into a tall glass and serve at once
with drinking straws.

Gingerbread shake

2 tbsp smooth caramel
  cookie spread
  (such as Lotus Biscoff)
100 ml/3⅓ oz. double/
  heavy cream
4 scoops vanilla ice
  cream
1 tbsp gingerbread syrup
250 ml/1 cup milk
  of your choice
multicoloured festive
  sprinkles, to decorate
mini gingerbread men or
  Lotus Biscoff cookies,
  to serve

blender
paper drinking straws
sundae spoon

SERVES 1

*All the flavours of Christmas Gingerbread in a glass
plus the rich caramel tones of moreish Lotus Biscoff
cookies. Serve with your choice of crunchy cookie
and decorate with colourful sprinkles for a cute iced
gingerbread house look.*

Prepare the caramel whipped cream topping first. Place
1 tablespoon of the caramel cookie spread and the cream
in a bowl and whisk gently to soft peaks. Chill until you are
ready to serve the drink.

Place 3 scoops of the ice cream, the gingerbread syrup, milk
and remaining caramel biscuit spread in a blender and blend
until smooth. Pour into a tall glass and top with the remaining
scoop of ice cream and the caramel whipped cream topping.

Decorate with sprinkles and serve at once with your choice
of cookie, drinking straws and a sundae spoon.

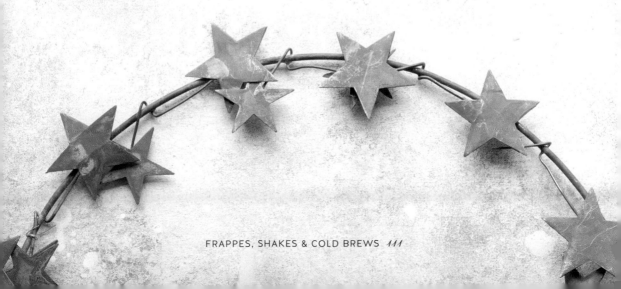

Festive freakshake

300 ml/1¼ cups milk
   of your choice
4 scoops strawberry
   ice cream
1 tbsp vanilla syrup,
   (see page 12) (optional)
1 tbsp chocolate sauce
   (see page 15)
100 ml/3⅓ oz. double/
   heavy cream, whipped
   to stiff peaks

TO ASSEMBLE
mini marshmallows
25 g/1 oz. good-quality
   white chocolate, melted
festive sprinkles
mini sugar doughnuts/
   donuts
candy floss/cotton candy

1 bamboo skewer, about
   10 cm/4 in. taller than
   your glass (fun ones
   if you can find them!)
blender
paper drinking straws
sundae spoon

SERVES 1

This is not a shake to make every day (particularly if you are calorie conscious!) but it is perfect for a special occasion and when I do serve this, it is universally loved. You can go wild and top with anything you like – cookies and brownies all work well, but I just love the combination of mini doughnuts/donuts and candy floss/cotton candy as it reminds me of fun fairs.

Prepare the marshmallow skewer first. Thread mini marshmallows onto the skewer, measuring so that the marshmallows will be above the surface of your drink when placed in the glass. Drizzle with thin lines of the melted chocolate and decorate with sprinkles. Place on a plate or small tray and put in the refrigerator.

Place the milk, three scoops of the strawberry ice cream and the vanilla syrup, if using, in a blender and blitz until you have a smooth shake and all the ice cream and milk have blended.

Drizzle wiggly lines of chocolate sauce into a tall, heavy-based serving glass and pour in the shake. Top with the whipped cream and the remaining scoop of ice cream.

Place mini sugar doughnuts on top, decorate with candy floss/cotton candy and the prepared marshmallow skewer and serve at once with drinking straws and a sundae spoon. Remember to tell whoever is drinking that the marshmallows are on a stick so they do not hurt their teeth!

Eggnog shake

1 caramel cookie,
  such as Lotus Biscoff,
  crushed to fine crumbs
  with a rolling pin
½ tbsp chocolate sauce
  (see page 15)
60 ml/¼ cup Advocaat
  liqueur, plus extra
  to taste and to drizzle
3 scoops of vanilla
  ice cream
200 ml/¾ cup milk
  of your choice
1 tbsp whipped double/
  heavy cream

blender
paper drinking straws

SERVES 1

Eggnog is such a traditional Christmas tipple that it would be remiss not to include a frozen version. It's perfect to serve over the festive season as an adult 'boozy shake'. Make sure you use good-quality vanilla ice cream as this will really make a difference to the flavour.

Prepare a serving glass first. Place the cookie crumbs on a plate. Place the chocolate sauce on another plate and carefully roll the rim of the glass in the chocolate. Roll the chocolate dipped rim in the crumbs until the chocolate is coated. Save the leftover crumbs to sprinkle over the drink. Set the glass aside until you are ready to serve.

Place the Advocaat, ice cream and milk in a blender and blitz until all the ice cream is blended into the milk. Taste and if you want a boozier shake, add more Advocaat. Pour into the prepared glass taking care not to pour onto the decorated rim. Top the glass with the whipped cream and sprinkle over a few of the leftover cookie crumbs and a drizzle of Advocaat. Serve at once with drinking straws.

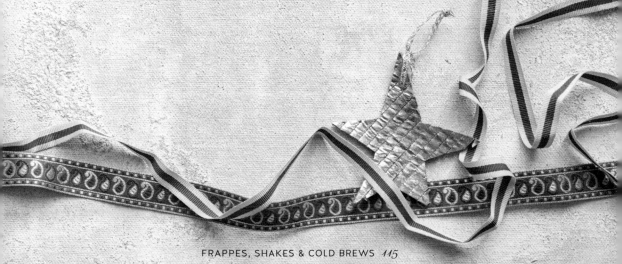

Cold brew espresso martini

75 ml/¹⁄₃ cup vodka

75 ml/¹⁄₃ cup coffee liqueur, such as Kahlua or Tia Maria, or coffee tequila

100 ml/scant ¹⁄₂ cup cold brew coffee (see page 9)

a generous handful of ice cubes

1 tbsp vanilla syrup (see page 12) or storebought simple syrup

chocolate-coated coffee beans, to garnish

cocktail shaker
2 martini/cocktail glasses, chilled

SERVES 2

If we are somewhere with espresso martini on the menu, it will always be the cocktail I select – it's the perfect drink for any night owl as it gives you the energy for a few more hours of dancing. For Christmas parties, you can serve this coffee tipple for your guests – it uses cold brew rather than espresso but still has a good caffeine hit and you can prepare the cold brew a day or so before the party, which saves you the rather impractical job of making lots of fresh espresso coffees on the night! I like to make this with a coffee tequila.

Place the vodka, coffee or tequila liqueur, cold brew coffee, ice cubes and syrup in a cocktail shaker and shake vigorously for a good few minutes. You want to shake it well to create a foamy layer on top of the cocktail when it is poured.

Pour into two chilled martini glasses, top each drink with three chocolate-coated coffee beans and serve at once.

Irish cream cold brew

100 ml/scant ⅓ cup
cold brew coffee
(see page 9)
handful of crushed ice
3 tbsp Irish cream syrup
(see below)
200 ml/¾ cup milk
of your choice
60 ml/¼ cup double/
heavy cream
cocoa powder, to dust

IRISH CREAM SYRUP
200 g/1 cup caster/white
granulated sugar
1 tsp vanilla bean powder
or vanilla extract
1 tsp almond extract
1 heaped tbsp cocoa
powder, sifted

balloon whisk
sterilized bottle or jar
(see page 4)
blender
paper drinking straws
sundae spoon

SERVES 1

I cannot sing the praises of cold brew coffee enough. It became hugely popular a few years ago and remains so today. It never ceases to amaze me just how much smooth coffee flavour is extracted by steeping crushed beans in cold water. The basic recipe for making cold brew is on page 9. You could of course make this Irish Cream coffee with an Irish Cream liqueur if you want a boozy tipple but for a morning coffee, try this Irish cream syrup which only takes a few minutes to prepare and tastes just like the real thing. You can store the leftover syrup in a sterilized bottle or jar in the refrigerator for up to one week.

Start by making the Irish cream syrup as this needs to cool completely before being used. Place the sugar and 250 ml/1 cup water in a pan with the vanilla bean powder or extract and almond extract and simmer until the sugar has dissolved. Add the cocoa and whisk well so that all the cocoa is incorporated into the syrup and there are no lumps. Pass through a sieve/strainer and leave to cool completely. Once cool poor into a sterilized bottle or jar and refrigerate.

When you are ready to serve, place the cold brew coffee, crushed ice and 1 tablespoon of the Irish cream syrup in a blender and blitz to crush the ice. Pour into a glass and top up with cold milk.

Place the cream and 2 tablespoons of the Irish cream syrup in a bowl and whisk to very soft peaks. Spoon on top of the coffee and dust with a little cocoa powder. Serve at once with drinking straws and a sundae spoon to stir in the cream.

Cookies & cream shake

4 scoops cookies
& cream ice cream
400 ml/1¾ cups milk
of your choice
2 tbsp chocolate sauce
(see page 15) or
storebought chocolate
syrup
5 Oreo cookies
whipped cream
(canned is fine)

paper drinking straws
sundae spoons

SERVES 2

Cookies & Cream – the hugely popular ice cream flavour – is the inspiration for this indulgent shake. Packed full of Oreo cookies and served with extra cookies on the side, it is naughty but oh, so nice. You can substitute store-bought chocolate syrup for the homemade chocolate sauce if you want to rustle this up at short notice!

Put two scoops of the ice cream in a blender with the milk, chocolate sauce or syrup and three of the Oreo cookies. Whizz until the shake is foamy and thick.

Pour into two tall glasses and top each with a scoop of ice cream. Add a small amount of whipped cream on top of each shake and decorate with Oreo crumbs and an Oreo cookie.

Serve at once with drinking straws and sundae spoons.

Christmas morning cold brew

50 g/½ cup coffee beans

1 cinnamon stick

3 whole cloves

½ tsp vanilla bean powder

zest of 1 orange, removed using a zester to make long strands of peel

a little freshly grated nutmeg

TO SERVE

long cinnamon stick, to stir (optional)

dried orange slice

sugar, to taste (optional)

blender

lidded container with approx. 500-ml/2-cups capacity

muslin or coffee filter paper

fine mesh sieve/strainer

MAKES 400 ML/1¾ CUPS

In the run up to Christmas, why not blitz up this spiced cold brew coffee, which only takes a few minutes to prepare but after 24 hours steeping has delicious hints of festive spices with mellow coffee notes. Drink it chilled or warm to wash down a slice of Christmas cake or a mince pie. If you do not have vanilla bean powder you can substitute vanilla bean paste or vanilla extract but add this with the water rather than to the blender for blitzing.

Place the coffee beans, cinnamon stick, cloves, vanilla, orange zest and nutmeg in a blender and blitz for a few seconds so that the beans are coarsely ground. Do not grind to a fine powder otherwise this will make the coffee have an unpleasant texture. Place in a lidded container and pour over 400 ml/1¾ cups water and stir with a spoon. Put the lid on the container and place in the refrigerator for 24 hours to steep.

Remove from the refrigerator and strain through a muslin or alternatively use a coffee filter in a fine mesh sieve/strainer. Make sure that all the coffee grounds are removed. The coffee is ready to serve once strained but can be stored in the refrigerator for up to 3 days (you can store for a few more days but the flavour will not be as good and as the coffee is quick to prepare it is best to make in smaller batches for the amount you need).

To serve, pour into an ice-filled tumbler and garnish with a cinnamon stick and dried orange slice.

Note: If you prefer a sweet coffee add a little sugar to taste and dissolve before serving or if you want the whole batch of coffee to be sweet, then add a tablespoon of sugar when you add the water before steeping.

Coffee ice cream frappé

2 shots (60 ml/2 oz.)
  freshly brewed
  espresso coffee, cooled
350 ml/1½ cups milk
  of your choice
4 scoops coffee ice
  cream
a large handful
  of crushed ice
whipped cream
  (canned is fine)
cocoa powder, for
  dusting
chocolate-coated
  coffee beans, to
  decorate

blender
paper drinking straws
sundae spoons

SERVES 2

*This milkshake is the ultimate pick-me-up – strong
coffee and sweet coffee ice cream. Coffee ice cream
is widely available and extremely delicious! But if you
can't find it, you can use vanilla ice cream and simply
add an extra shot of espresso.*

Put the cooled espresso, milk and two scoops of the coffee
ice cream in a blender with the crushed ice and blitz until
thick and creamy.

Pour the shake into the two tall glasses and top each glass
with a scoop of coffee ice cream. Squirt a little of the cream
on top of the shake, dust with cocoa powder and top with
chocolate coffee beans. Serve at once with drinking straws
and sundae spoons.

Index

Acknowledgements

Thank you hugely to the wonderful RPS team for this stunning and yummy book, particularly to Julia Charles my amazing friend for commissioning the book and allowing me to indulge my love of festive drinks. A particular thank you to Leslie Harrington and Toni Kay for the wonderful design. Thanks also go to Alex Luck for the beautiful photography, and to Lorna Brash and Luis peral for bringing such flair to the food and prop styling. Heather, Elly and Rob at HHB, thank you for all your valued help and support over the many years we have worked together. To my friends Jess and Millie for the 250-mile round trip to deliver toffee-nut latte syrup in the middle of summer and for sparing your rations – I will be eternally grateful. With love and thanks to all my family and friends who support me all along the way and who enjoyed the early festive drinks – Katie, my Mum and Dad, Liz and Mike, Gareth and Amy, Lucy and David, Maren, Charlotte, Aiden, Debs, Taffy, Kathy and Simon – you all mean the world to me!

The publishers wish to thank KitchenAid™ (kitchenaid.co.uk) for the loan of an espresso machine and Toogood (t-o-o-g-o-o-d.com) for the loan of props.

RECIPE CREDITS

All recipes Hannah Miles, with the exception of pages 58, 61, 62 and 74 Louise Pickford.

Please note some recipes in this book have been previously published by Ryland Peters & Small in *Milkshake Bar* (2012) and *Hot Chocolate* (2015) both by Hannah Miles.

PICTURE CREDITS

All photography by Alex Luck with the following exceptions:

Steve Painter Pages 39, 68, 69, 70, 73, 77, 78, 82, 85, 86, 87, 89, 93, 94, 96, 97, 98 and 120.

Clare Winfield Pages 27, 31, 43, 48, 63, 88, 103, 111, 115 and 124.

Peter Cassidy Pages 3, 19, 20, 28, 76, 80, 104, 108 and 128.

Kate Whitaker Pages 59, 92 and 95.

Adrian Lawrence Pages 23 and 52.

William Lingwood Pages 67 and 83.

William Reavell Page 44.

Jan Baldwin Page 72.

Ian Wallace Page 60.